More Whispers From Your Soul™

Hear what you really need to hear...

© 2014 God c/o A. Drayton Boylston

Copyright © 2014 by A. Drayton Boylston.

All rights reserved under International and Pan-American Copyright Conventions. No part of this book may be reproduced or transmitted in any form or by any means, electronic or mechanical, including photocopying, recording, or by any other storage and retrieval system, without written permission from the publisher.

Coming UnScrooged and Save Yourself From The Life You've Created are registered trademarks with the United States Copyright and Patent Office. Corporate Vortex, A Short Guide to Corporate Rescue, and Rescue Institute, are trademarks owned by A. Drayton Boylston. Rescue Institute Publishing and its trademark are trademarks of the Rescue Institute.

The Author and Publisher specifically disclaim any liability, loss, or risk that is incurred as a consequence, directly or indirectly, of the use and application of any of the contents of this work.

Publishers Cataloging-in-Publication Data

Boylston, A. Drayton.

A Whisper From Your Soul- Hear what you really need to hear.

/ A. Drayton Boylston. —Golden, Colo.: Rescue Institute Publishing, 2014.

p. ; cm.

ISBN-13: 978-0-9749314-1-8

ISBN-10: 0-9749314-1-1

1. Personal Development—United States—Fiction. 2. Corporate Culture—United States—Fiction. 3. Organizational Change—United States—Fiction.

I. Title.

PS3602.O957 C66 2006

813.6—dc22   0603

Edited by Jennifer-Crystal Johnson

www.jennifercrystaljohnson.com

Printed in the U.S.A.
First Edition

HB Printing 10 9 8 7 6 5 4 3 2 1

Please visit our websites:

www.WhisperFromYourSoul.com

www.DraytonBoylston.com

www.ExecutiveCoachingUniversity.com

Please call for bulk purchase discounts: 1.800.251.1696.

Also by A. Drayton Boylston

- A Whisper From Your Soul
- Coming UnScrooged! A Contemporary Classic of Corporate Rescue and Redemption
- The Life Purpose Workbook
- The Sage and Scholars Guide to Coaching Executives
- Rescued Executive Series:
    - Coach as Lifeguard
    - Executive CPR
    - Coach as EMT
- Rescued Executive Chronicles
- Whispers From Your Soul Blog

To sign up for *A Whisper From Your Soul* email program please visit:

www.DraytonBoylston.com

Table of Contents

- What People are Saying About the *Whispers*
- Why *More* Whispers?
- Loving Guidance
- The Whispers
- About Drayton
- Resources

What People are Saying about the Whispers...

"A Whisper From Your Soul is an inspirational book that will touch your soul and heart more than you can ever imagine. Each daily thought will stir a response, challenging us to embrace it, moving forward with a sense of peace and joy."

"A must-have book! No matter where you are or what you do, this book will touch you at your deepest level. It has been a long time since I have felt the power of a book like I did with this one."

"I recently purchased this for myself for the New Year as a daily way to 'inspire' my soul to better things. I also purchased a few for friends. One friend, upon receiving this, was moved to tears with Drayton's words."

"I so enjoyed the simple yet profound impact this book has had on me. It is a needed breath of fresh air and a way to stay grounded in what is truly

important in life. I plan on giving this to everyone I love as a gift."

"A Whisper for Your Soul is a collection of wise and perceptive observations that move, encourage, and invite the reader to look at and live daily life from a new, wider perspective of freedom and generosity of spirit."

"A great reminder of what is important in life. Should be required reading by all leaders and anyone in a position of being a role model (everyone)."

"A beautiful, spiritually motivating daily devotional! A must-read for all on their spiritual journey!!!"

"It's a great daily read that lasts all year. It's habit forming; you cannot go a day without picking it up for inspiration. Terrific book!"

"This book is inspiring and contains real truths that one should read and grow from. What a great reminder to listen to our still, quiet voice. This is a MUST-READ!"

Why More Whispers?

Phew! What a trip it has been since I wrote the original *Whispers*. The story that unfolded after I finished writing the book was nothing short of breathtaking. Here's what happened.

If you read the original *Whispers* (if you didn't, why not? ☺) you know that I felt inspired to write the book as a tribute to my late Mom. Each Christmas she would give me a new daily devotional book to use in the coming year. This beautiful gift laid the foundation for many things in my life. From encouraging me to take time to be thoughtful to appreciating the value of serving others, it was so very beneficial.

I knew that I wanted to write the *Whispers* and also knew that I would do it… someday.

During December of 2012 I received a *"Divine nudge"* that *"now"* was *"someday."*

That December I realized that my aunt, my Mom's sister, was turning 90 years old. While she was in good health, I felt divinely inspired to accelerate my timeline and finish the *Whispers* before Christmas so that I could give it to her as a Birthday/Christmas present.

"Sister," as we call her, is a highly spiritual being who has been a big influence on my spiritual journey. She has been deeply immersed in spiritual teaching her entire adult life and has traveled to most of the world's holy sites. I desperately wanted her to have a copy of the *Whispers*... quickly.

So I sped up production (I had to write over 100 Whispers in just a few days) and set the goal of getting a hard copy of the *Whispers* to Sister by Christmas.

Well, the stars aligned and we (I am blessed with terrific folks who helped me) made it happen. Yippee!

This is where it got interesting. You see, the *Whispers* were never meant to be a commercial endeavor. It was a simple, heartfelt tribute to Mom. Nothing more.

I decided to print a few copies for family and friends. At the last minute, I also decided to put it on Amazon so family and friends could order more copies if they wanted to.

What happened next was nothing short of a miracle….

Within 24 hours of being posted on Amazon, with ZERO marketing, the *Whispers* took off! It skyrocketed 845,000 places overnight. Within a few days it was ranked in the top 0.5% of all books on Amazon. That is out of over 6 million books!

Let me repeat, this was without ANY marketing plan and budget.

Wouldn't you say that's a miracle?!

The feedback I've received from folks has been so humbling. From a Catholic Bishop who says that he consults the *Whispers* every morning to start his day to an executive who said it has changed his life in a most profound way, the response has truly fed my soul.

Sooooo…

That is why I decided to write *More Whispers From Your Soul.*

I hope it brings you as much joy as it did me as I was given these words. Please know that these words are offered with love and a supreme desire to serve you as best I can.

I offer these usage suggestions as I did in the original *Whispers:*

As you read each page, take some time to write down whatever thoughts come up for you and let them simply emerge; they may feel random, off topic, or maybe even a bit bizarre. Know that these are simply judgments that are good to move past. Let your words and resulting feelings simply flow. This will help in ways that I can't describe with words. Please give yourself this gift.

Know that you are loved, more than you can ever imagine. Know that joy is yours each and every day; you only need to choose it and revel in the fact that you have everything that you need right now.

Indeed, blessings abound!

Wishing you peace, joy, and love!

Loving Guidance

The beautiful thing about the *Whispers* is that it is so much more than just the words you see on the pages. It is about the words that you *will* see on the pages... those heartfelt *Whispers* that *you* add yourself.

I have made some formatting changes to this new edition of the *Whispers* that I wanted to bring to your attention. This is based on some wonderful feedback from a large number of readers.

Many folks felt that they *had* to start at the beginning of the year and also felt a bit of stress if they missed a day. I certainly do not want anyone to feel *any* stress as they use this resource. Quite the opposite.

So....

I have elected to take out the dates on each page. This frees you up to start anywhere! You can simply open your *Whispers* to any page that feels right. Where you read and write is up to you… just as it should be. You can start at any time of the year.

Also, you will find another change to this edition of the *Whispers*. I have added a number of *"exercises."* The goal is to provide *"prompts"* that will encourage you to dig even deeper with your *own Whispers*.

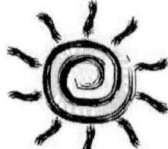

Are you curious about this symbol you see on each page? It is very special.

This is the Native American symbol for happiness. This is what I wish for you as you embark on each day.

Enjoy!

With love,

Dedication

To my dear family – Kathryn, Taylor, and Adam.

You are the greatest gifts

I have ever been blessed with.

The Whispers

How will your life be different one year from today?
Your thoughts...

_____
_____
_____
_____
_____

How might you love more?
Your thoughts...

_____
_____
_____
_____
_____

What one thing do you need to forgive yourself for?
Your thoughts...

_____
_____
_____
_____
_____

How old would you be if no one ever told you?
Your thoughts...

_____
_____
_____
_____
_____

Someday isn't a day of the week.

Your thoughts...

___

What have you become?

Your thoughts...

___

Live in reverence of every moment.
Your thoughts...

_____
_____
_____
_____
_____

Your outside world simply reflects your inside world.
Your thoughts...

_____
_____
_____
_____
_____

There are no differences... only judgments.

Your thoughts...

_____

_____

_____

_____

_____

Pick one old friend to call today.

Your thoughts...

_____

_____

_____

_____

_____

True wealth is never measured in the currency of this world.

Your thoughts...

_____
_____
_____
_____
_____

Meditation leads to manifestation.

Your thoughts...

_____
_____
_____
_____
_____

Remember... you chose this life.

Your thoughts...

_____

_____

_____

_____

_____

It's never been about you.

Your thoughts...

_____

_____

_____

_____

_____

Become a "*Chatter Boxer*" with your negative self-talk.
Your thoughts...

_____
_____
_____
_____
_____

Choose what media you let into your head.
Your thoughts...

_____
_____
_____
_____
_____

You are never really present with a phone in your hand.
Your thoughts...

_____
_____
_____
_____
_____

Smiling bridges all gaps.
Your thoughts...

_____
_____
_____
_____
_____

List three things you love about yourself.
Your thoughts…

_____
_____
_____
_____
_____

Hugging is the best therapy.
Your thoughts…

_____
_____
_____
_____
_____

No pill can do what you can do naturally.

Your thoughts...

_____

_____

_____

_____

_____

Any vice = avoidance.

Your thoughts...

_____

_____

_____

_____

_____

Observe your thoughts as if they were traffic on a busy road.
Your thoughts...

_____
_____
_____
_____
_____

Three deep breaths dispel all stress.
Your thoughts...

_____
_____
_____
_____
_____

Lead... don't impede.
Your thoughts...

_____
_____
_____
_____
_____

L.O.V.E. - Let Our Village Embrace
Your thoughts...

_____
_____
_____
_____
_____

Making a buck doesn't compare to making a difference.
Your thoughts…

_____
_____
_____
_____
_____

What happens to one happens to all.
Your thoughts…

_____
_____
_____
_____
_____

What did you want to be as a child? Why?
Your thoughts...

_____
_____
_____
_____
_____

A society that is sick needs to acknowledge its illness before seeking a cure.
Your thoughts...

_____
_____
_____
_____
_____
_____

Do you feel "the shift?" It starts with you....
Your thoughts...

_____

_____

_____

_____

_____

Silence = Awareness
Your thoughts...

_____

_____

_____

_____

_____

You can never run out of love.

Your thoughts…

_____

_____

_____

_____

_____

Make all of your goals internal, not external.

Your thoughts…

_____

_____

_____

_____

_____

Take ownership of your life. You own it... no one else.
Your thoughts...

_____
_____
_____
_____
_____

Miracles happen when we replace blame with bless.
Your thoughts...

_____
_____
_____
_____

It's not about money... it's about you!
Your thoughts...

_____
_____
_____
_____
_____

There are many paths to the truth.
Your thoughts...

_____
_____
_____
_____
_____

Who can you send a thank you note to today?

Your thoughts...

_____

_____

_____

_____

_____

Knowledge is not wisdom.

Your thoughts...

_____

_____

_____

_____

_____

Inspired action is from your soul. All other action is from your ego.
Your thoughts...

_____

_____

_____

_____

_____

E.G.O. ~ Eventually Growing Obsolete
Your thoughts...

_____

_____

_____

_____

_____

If you stay in the "*now*" you will always find the "*how.*"

Your thoughts...

_____

_____

_____

_____

_____

True abundance is never measured on a balance sheet.

Your thoughts...

_____

_____

_____

_____

Imagine if... you weren't your body.
Your thoughts...

_____
_____
_____
_____
_____

What if you treated each breath as a gift?
Your thoughts...

_____
_____
_____
_____
_____

Stress is a choice.
Your thoughts...

_____

_____

_____

_____

_____

Call one of your relatives today and tell them you love them.
Your thoughts...

_____

_____

_____

_____

_____

If you own it, act on it. If you don't, let it go.
Your thoughts…

_____
_____
_____
_____
_____

Suffering is always optional.
Your thoughts…

_____
_____
_____
_____
_____

The Plan is perfect... so are you!
Your thoughts...

_____

_____

_____

_____

_____

You create your circumstances with your thoughts.
Your thoughts...

_____

_____

_____

_____

_____

You are a force of nature... exercise your power!

Your thoughts...

_____
_____
_____
_____
_____

When in doubt, choose Spirit!

Your thoughts...

_____
_____
_____
_____
_____

True spiritual growth is not about you… it's about others.
Your thoughts…

_____

_____

_____

_____

_____

Dis-ease is not about your body.
Your thoughts…

_____

_____

_____

_____

_____

Write a note to your younger self, passing on some lessons you've learned.
Your thoughts...

_____

_____

_____

_____

_____

Pssst... here's a secret: you can totally remake yourself today!
Your thoughts...

_____

_____

_____

_____

Drama attracts drama.

Your thoughts...

___

Learn to simply observe your thoughts.

Your thoughts...

___

When you change, everyone around you changes.
Your thoughts...

_____
_____
_____
_____
_____

Your "vibe" sets the tone for everything.
Your thoughts...

_____
_____
_____
_____
_____

Slay stress with silence.
Your thoughts...

_____
_____
_____
_____
_____

All that you see around you at this very moment is a reflection of what is going on inside you.
Your thoughts...

_____
_____
_____
_____

True learning exists in your heart, not your head.

Your thoughts…

_____

_____

_____

_____

_____

Lead fearlessly with your heart.

Your thoughts…

_____

_____

_____

_____

_____

List one thing you are avoiding and what you will do about it.
Your thoughts...

_____
_____
_____
_____
_____

When you meet anyone, act as if you are related... because you are.
Your thoughts...

_____
_____
_____
_____

Declare "*who*" and "*what*" you are out loud a few times a day.
Your thoughts...

_____
_____
_____
_____
_____

Your "*to be*" state is already a reality.
Your thoughts...

_____
_____
_____
_____
_____

Money is only an issue for you, not the Universe.
Your thoughts...

___

Say "*I love you*" ten times a day... to yourself.
Your thoughts...

___

None of your so-called "*problems*" reside outside of you.
Your thoughts…

_____
_____
_____
_____
_____

Set your goals for today, not the year.
Your thoughts…

_____
_____
_____
_____
_____

Striving doesn't lead to getting.
Your thoughts…

_____
_____
_____
_____
_____

You can't "*get*" anything… you already have it.
Your thoughts…

_____
_____
_____
_____
_____

Name one way you can give back today.
Your thoughts…

___

"*Why me?*" should not be in your vocabulary.
Your thoughts…

You are loved by so many in such a deep way...
love yourself the same way.
Your thoughts...

_____

_____

_____

_____

_____

You are not your body.
Your thoughts...

_____

_____

_____

_____

_____

List one so-called "*weakness*" that you can turn into an opportunity.
Your thoughts...

_____

_____

_____

_____

_____

A dream life has nothing to do with anything outside of you.
Your thoughts...

_____

_____

_____

_____

Free Will means that you have complete ownership of your life.
Your thoughts...

_____

_____

_____

_____

_____

How can you thank a former teacher of yours?
Your thoughts...

_____

_____

_____

_____

_____

No one can "*make you*" anything. You choose
what to be and how to react.
Your thoughts...

_____
_____
_____
_____
_____

Look in the mirror today and say "*I am loved*"
ten times.
Your thoughts...

_____
_____
_____
_____

Anger is simply your ego winning.
Your thoughts...

_____
_____
_____
_____
_____

Our human connection can never be broken.
Your thoughts...

_____
_____
_____
_____
_____

You are only as popular as you think you are.
Your thoughts...

_____
_____
_____
_____
_____

Living "*the dream*" is a daily choice and only requires your thoughts to achieve.
Your thoughts...

_____
_____
_____
_____
_____

You don't have any weaknesses... only opportunities.
Your thoughts...

_____

_____

_____

_____

_____

Saying, "How may I serve?" will make every conversation better.
Your thoughts...

_____

_____

_____

_____

List three of your greatest strengths. How are you using them?
Your thoughts...

_____

_____

_____

_____

_____

The Universe doesn't revolve around you... it *is* you.
Your thoughts...

_____

_____

_____

_____

Since God made you... you are part of God too.

Your thoughts...

_____
_____
_____
_____
_____

You will never be in a place where God isn't.

Your thoughts...

_____
_____
_____
_____

You created your current circumstances. Own it.
Your thoughts…

_____
_____
_____
_____
_____

Whenever you are in doubt, just close your eyes and count your breaths for ten seconds.
Your thoughts…

_____
_____
_____
_____

Embrace that we are all from the same Source and all perceived differences will disappear.
Your thoughts...

_____
_____
_____
_____
_____

Note three reasons why you are on this planet.
Your thoughts...

_____
_____
_____
_____
_____

You are surrounded by more love than you can comprehend in human form.
Your thoughts...

_____

_____

_____

_____

_____

Your body is simply a vessel for this mission.
Your thoughts...

_____

_____

_____

_____

_____

What does trust mean to you?

Your thoughts...

___

___

___

___

___

Allow good things to come your way.

Your thoughts...

___

___

___

___

___

Always receive with a knowing smile.

Your thoughts...

_____

_____

_____

_____

_____

You can glimpse everyone's Soul in their eyes.

Your thoughts...

_____

_____

_____

_____

_____

Children are closest to God because they were most recently with Him. Treat them as the wise Souls they are.
Your thoughts...

_____
_____
_____
_____
_____

Politics only serve to polarize.
Your thoughts...

_____
_____
_____
_____

True love doesn't know borders, religion, politics, or any perceived differences.
Your thoughts…

_____
_____
_____
_____
_____

Focus on our common thread. All else is of man, not God.
Your thoughts…

_____
_____
_____
_____

Write down three weaknesses you have on a piece of paper. Now... rip it to shreds!
Your thoughts...

_____
_____
_____
_____
_____

Tell someone they are beautiful today... and really mean it.
Your thoughts...

_____
_____
_____
_____

You are beautiful!
Your thoughts...

_____
_____
_____
_____
_____

All of your relationships are a reflection of the relationship you have with yourself.
Your thoughts...

_____
_____
_____
_____
_____

Remember... you are the only one listening
when you talk to yourself.
Your thoughts...

_____
_____
_____
_____
_____

You are home wherever you are.
Your thoughts...

_____
_____
_____
_____
_____

God knows... yes, *you* do.
Your thoughts...

_____
_____
_____
_____
_____

You are like a present... the wrapping is all the world sees, yet the real gift is inside.
Your thoughts...

_____
_____
_____
_____
_____

Fill in the blank... God is

_____.

Your thoughts...

_____
_____
_____
_____
_____

Close your eyes for five minutes and simply count your breaths.

Your thoughts...

_____
_____
_____
_____

Your intuition is God's messenger.

Your thoughts…

_____
_____
_____
_____
_____

Deep human connection requires no words.

Your thoughts…

_____
_____
_____
_____
_____

A hug will heal many wounds.
Your thoughts...

_____
_____
_____
_____
_____

You are what you think you are... or aren't.
Your thoughts...

_____
_____
_____
_____
_____

Think of the person you love most in the world.
Now show that love to yourself.
Your thoughts...

_____
_____
_____
_____
_____

See yourself as your best friends see you.
Your thoughts...

_____
_____
_____
_____
_____

Your Soul is eternal. When your body ceases to be, it is simply the end of this chapter.
Your thoughts...

_____

_____

_____

_____

_____

It's not about being perfect... only present.
Your thoughts...

_____

_____

_____

_____

_____

Choose to speak only if it improves the silence.
Your thoughts…

_____
_____
_____
_____
_____

Write a love note to yourself.
Your thoughts…

_____
_____
_____
_____
_____

Y.O.U. - Your... Own... Universe.
Your thoughts...

_____
_____
_____
_____
_____

"*Why me?*" is a victim's refrain. Don't let it be yours.
Your thoughts...

_____
_____
_____
_____
_____

You were born with a mission. Your ego tries to convince you that you don't have one.
Your thoughts…

_____
_____
_____
_____
_____

We are closest to Spirit at birth.
Your thoughts…

_____
_____
_____
_____
_____

H.E.A.R.T. – Help Everyone Achieve Real Truth.
Your thoughts...

_____

_____

_____

_____

_____

Don't aspire to work. Aspire to serve.
Your thoughts...

_____

_____

_____

_____

_____

You own your career, not your boss.
Your thoughts...

_____
_____
_____
_____
_____

Strive to give first. Put "*getting*" out of your mind.
Your thoughts...

_____
_____
_____
_____
_____

We are all brothers and sisters connected in Spirit.
Your thoughts...

___

___

___

___

___

What is your greatest gift? How are you using it?
Your thoughts...

___

___

___

___

There are no "*less fortunate*" people. Only
people on different paths.
Your thoughts...

_____

_____

_____

_____

_____

You alone control your reality.
Your thoughts...

_____

_____

_____

_____

_____

Spirit shines its light through each person's eyes. Look for it in everyone you encounter.
Your thoughts...

_____

_____

_____

_____

_____

Choose a calling versus a career.
Your thoughts...

_____

_____

_____

_____

_____

There are no strangers. We all know each other on a deep level in another realm.
Your thoughts...

_____
_____
_____
_____
_____

Cause and effect are simply your thoughts manifested.
Your thoughts...

_____
_____
_____
_____

Playing it safe never leads to growth.
Your thoughts...

_____

_____

_____

_____

_____

You are what you think you are.
Your thoughts...

_____

_____

_____

_____

_____

Our path is already set. Our choice is how long it takes us to follow it.
Your thoughts…

_____
_____
_____
_____
_____

Do what scares you the most. Growth resides there.
Your thoughts…

_____
_____
_____
_____

Name one way you took inspired action today.
Your thoughts...

_____
_____
_____
_____
_____

Do the undone... always.
Your thoughts...

_____
_____
_____
_____
_____

Say the unsaid... always.

Your thoughts...

_____

_____

_____

_____

_____

Forgiveness breeds freedom.

Your thoughts...

_____

_____

_____

_____

_____

Treat everyone you encounter as someone famous… because they are.

Your thoughts…

_____

_____

_____

_____

_____

"*Being*" is really "*seeing.*"

Your thoughts…

_____

_____

_____

_____

_____

"*I am*" will create your reality.

Your thoughts…

_____

_____

_____

_____

_____

Striving for perfection is the ego's way of
keeping you out of the "*now.*"

Your thoughts…

_____

_____

_____

_____

_____

Gratitude... not platitudes.
Your thoughts...

_____
_____
_____
_____
_____

Who did you serve today? In what way?
Your thoughts...

_____
_____
_____
_____
_____

Your ego's goal is to keep your Soul in chains.
Your thoughts...

_____
_____
_____
_____
_____

Hearing the voice of your Soul is a choice.
Your thoughts...

_____
_____
_____
_____
_____

You carry your "*home*" with you wherever you go.
Your thoughts...

_____

_____

_____

_____

_____

Heaven is a choice, not a place.
Your thoughts...

_____

_____

_____

_____

_____

You don't go anywhere when you die, for you are already "*there.*"
Your thoughts...

_____

_____

_____

_____

_____

Misguided religion is a weapon of the ego.
Your thoughts...

_____

_____

_____

_____

_____

Once you realize that God is a part of you,
everything will make sense.
Your thoughts...

_____
_____
_____
_____
_____

Say hello to one "*stranger*" today.
Your thoughts...

_____
_____
_____
_____
_____

Man, not God, creates all pain.
Your thoughts…

_____
_____
_____
_____
_____

Always focus on similarities, not differences.
Your thoughts…

_____
_____
_____
_____
_____

Things are shifting toward love. How can you help accelerate this movement?
Your thoughts...

___

Judging always hurts you more than the person you judge.
Your thoughts...

It's not "*who*" you are... it's "*what*" you have become.
Your thoughts...

_____
_____
_____
_____
_____

Understand that your "*real*" family wouldn't fit under your roof.
Your thoughts...

_____
_____
_____
_____

Politics only serves man, not Spirit.
Your thoughts…

_____
_____
_____
_____
_____

Words are powerful weapons. Always use them with loving care.
Your thoughts…

_____
_____
_____
_____
_____

Name one person whom you really listened to today.
Your thoughts...

_____
_____
_____
_____
_____

We gain energy from each smile we pass on.
Your thoughts...

_____
_____
_____
_____
_____

Love is a well with no bottom.

Your thoughts...

___

___

___

___

___

C.A.R.E. ~ Create A Radical Experience!

Your thoughts...

___

___

___

___

___

Arriving is never achieved from striving.
Your thoughts...

___

Saying, "*I will*," triggers His.
Your thoughts...

There are 7 billion people on earth, each having a different experience. Respect all of them.

Your thoughts...

_____
_____
_____
_____
_____

Differences are of man, not God.

Your thoughts...

_____
_____
_____
_____

You are a prophet... you just haven't admitted it to yourself yet.
Your thoughts...

_____
_____
_____
_____
_____

List three things people will say about you at your funeral.
Your thoughts...

_____
_____
_____
_____

Spirit speaks to you 24/7. How many hours a day do you hear It?
Your thoughts...

___

Busy-ness is avoidance.
Your thoughts...

___

You are God's voice. Let His words speak through you.
Your thoughts...

_____

_____

_____

_____

_____

If God made you, why would you want to change anything?
Your thoughts...

_____

_____

_____

_____

Embrace prosperity.
Your thoughts...

_____

_____

_____

_____

_____

We determine our own Heaven and Hell.
Your thoughts...

_____

_____

_____

_____

_____

The road to success is never an interstate.

Your thoughts…

_____
_____
_____
_____
_____

Note three reasons why people love you.

Your thoughts…

_____
_____
_____
_____
_____

Love like a maniac!

Your thoughts…

_____

_____

_____

_____

_____

Each breath is God breathing life into you.

Cherish each one.

Your thoughts…

_____

_____

_____

_____

_____

If you feel inspired to take any kind of action,
always do so.
Your thoughts...

_____

_____

_____

_____

_____

Free Will is God's way of giving us ownership
of our path.
Your thoughts...

_____

_____

_____

_____

At birth, we know. We spend the rest of our lives seeking this Truth. At death, we remember....
Your thoughts...

_____
_____
_____
_____
_____

All paths lead to God. Respect each of them.
Your thoughts...

_____
_____
_____
_____

Give five compliments today... and every day.
Your thoughts...

_____
_____
_____
_____
_____

When you see differences in others, you create a separation from God.
Your thoughts...

_____
_____
_____
_____
_____

Silence is like swimming in God's reservoir.
Your thoughts...

_____

_____

_____

_____

_____

Close your eyes. Yep, He is there.
Your thoughts...

_____

_____

_____

_____

_____

Forgive one person today.
Your thoughts…

_____
_____
_____
_____
_____

Curiosity leads to growth.
Your thoughts…

_____
_____
_____
_____
_____

Speak your "*peace.*"
Your thoughts...

_____
_____
_____
_____
_____

Give the gift of sincere listening as much as you can.
Your thoughts...

_____
_____
_____
_____
_____

Revere kindness.
Your thoughts…

_____
_____
_____
_____
_____

Name three people whom you really connected with today.
Your thoughts…

_____
_____
_____
_____
_____

Embrace so-called "*quirkiness.*"
Your thoughts...

_____
_____
_____
_____
_____

Rejoice in your journey... this is the ultimate gift.
Your thoughts...

_____
_____
_____
_____
_____

The Universe does not give tests.
Your thoughts…

_____
_____
_____
_____
_____

Hell is living by listening to your ego.
Your thoughts…

_____
_____
_____
_____
_____

Your choice of friends reflects your self-image.
Your thoughts...

_____
_____
_____
_____
_____

Tell yourself, "*I am open to receiving.*"
Your thoughts...

_____
_____
_____
_____
_____

God is democratic... and it has nothing to do with politics.
Your thoughts...

_____
_____
_____
_____
_____

Grace is forgiving someone who is trying to harm you.
Your thoughts...

_____
_____
_____
_____

When you react with anger, you give your power away.
Your thoughts...

___

What one thing can you do right now to be more present?
Your thoughts...

Only five inches separates you from greatness... the space between your ears.
Your thoughts...

_____

_____

_____

_____

_____

You are not your brain. You are the observer of its thoughts.
Your thoughts...

_____

_____

_____

_____

If your body is busy, make sure the real you isn't.

Your thoughts…

_____
_____
_____
_____
_____

No one's opinion matters… but yours.

Your thoughts…

_____
_____
_____
_____
_____

"Doing" edges out *"Being."*
Your thoughts...

_____

_____

_____

_____

_____

List three reasons why you are happy.
Your thoughts...

_____

_____

_____

_____

_____

"*Still*" lets in His will.
Your thoughts...

_____
_____
_____
_____
_____

Embrace you.
Your thoughts...

_____
_____
_____
_____
_____

Anytime we lash out, it is against ourselves.
Your thoughts…

_____
_____
_____
_____
_____

Everything you desire is waiting for you.
Your thoughts…

_____
_____
_____
_____
_____

Strive to be imperfect... because there is nothing else.
Your thoughts...

_____

_____

_____

_____

_____

Embrace discomfort. That's where growth resides.
Your thoughts...

_____

_____

_____

_____

Note three ways you took care of yourself today.
Your thoughts...

_____
_____
_____
_____
_____

Always speak without words first.
Your thoughts...

_____
_____
_____
_____
_____

Be inspired... in *spirit*.
Your thoughts...

_____
_____
_____
_____
_____

Choose to listen first.
Your thoughts...

_____
_____
_____
_____
_____

List three highlights of your day.
Your thoughts…

_____

_____

_____

_____

_____

If you are in a place of service, you will never be taken advantage of.
Your thoughts…

_____

_____

_____

_____

_____

Never disagree. Seek to be curious.
Your thoughts...

_____
_____
_____
_____
_____

In each ray of light resides a message from God.
Your thoughts...

_____
_____
_____
_____
_____

Embrace the elderly. They are closer to the Truth.
Your thoughts…

_____

_____

_____

_____

_____

Growing old is simply climbing the ladder to Heaven.
Your thoughts…

_____

_____

_____

_____

Honor yourself first in order to honor others.
Your thoughts...

___

Hope is not a strategy.
Your thoughts...

Say, "I am grateful for all things," ten times a day.
Your thoughts...

_____
_____
_____
_____
_____

By repeating each day, "*Thy will be done,*" you will make it so.
Your thoughts...

_____
_____
_____
_____

Care for yourself... in order to care for others.

Your thoughts...

_____

_____

_____

_____

_____

Life is an "*inside*" game.

Your thoughts...

_____

_____

_____

_____

_____

Happiness can be found in every step of your journey.
Your thoughts...

_____

_____

_____

_____

_____

True gratitude is being grateful when things are going poorly.
Your thoughts...

_____

_____

_____

_____

Our reality is vastly different from how others perceive it.
Your thoughts…

___

___

___

___

___

"*I am___,*" is still the most powerful tool to change your life.
Your thoughts…

___

___

___

___

Heaven on earth is the message you were put here to spread.
Your thoughts...

_____
_____
_____
_____
_____

Describe your perfect day.
Your thoughts...

_____
_____
_____
_____
_____

Start enjoying your adventure today!
Your thoughts...

_____
_____
_____
_____
_____

Imagine if... absolutely everything was connected.
Your thoughts...

_____
_____
_____
_____
_____

Your skin is simply a sack for your Soul.
Your thoughts...

_____
_____
_____
_____
_____

Your Soul is God's calling card.
Your thoughts...

_____
_____
_____
_____
_____

Imagine your thoughts as a field of energy around you. Pick good ones.
Your thoughts...

_____

_____

_____

_____

_____

Duality is the ego's biggest lie.
Your thoughts...

_____

_____

_____

_____

_____

Failure only happens when you don't learn
from an experience.
Your thoughts…

_____
_____
_____
_____
_____

Declare three things that you deeply value.
Your thoughts…

_____
_____
_____
_____
_____

Aging simply means we are moving closer to our Source.
Your thoughts…

_____
_____
_____
_____
_____

Every single person has the same potential to help this planet.
Your thoughts…

_____
_____
_____
_____

Pick Blessed over Stressed.

Your thoughts...

_____
_____
_____
_____
_____

You are exactly what you think you are.

Your thoughts...

_____
_____
_____
_____
_____

Assume everyone is dealing with something tough.
Your thoughts...

_____
_____
_____
_____
_____

The road to success is dotted with learning pot holes.
Your thoughts...

_____
_____
_____
_____

A smile is addictive to those who see it.
Your thoughts...

_____
_____
_____
_____
_____

List three reasons why you are a hero.
Your thoughts...

_____
_____
_____
_____
_____

When in doubt, give a compliment.
Your thoughts...

_____
_____
_____
_____
_____

Denote the main reason you are alive.
Your thoughts...

_____
_____
_____
_____
_____

Remove "*not fair*" from your lexicon.

Your thoughts…

_____

_____

_____

_____

_____

Victims choose fear. Victors choose love.

Your thoughts…

_____

_____

_____

_____

_____

Worry is like a sinkhole.
Your thoughts…

_____

_____

_____

_____

_____

Love with wild abandon!
Your thoughts…

_____

_____

_____

_____

_____

Slow down....
Your thoughts...

_____
_____
_____
_____
_____

One kind word can change the trajectory of a person's journey.
Your thoughts...

_____
_____
_____
_____
_____

Purpose is not found. It is revealed.
Your thoughts...

_____
_____
_____
_____
_____

It's never a setback unless you see it that way.
Your thoughts...

_____
_____
_____
_____
_____

Own it!
Your thoughts...

_____
_____
_____
_____
_____

Pick one positive thought for today. Say it ten times during the day.
Your thoughts...

_____
_____
_____
_____
_____

Heaven resides between your ears.

Your thoughts...

_____

_____

_____

_____

_____

Your parents are not to blame.

Your thoughts...

_____

_____

_____

_____

_____

Choose your friends based on who you *want* to be.
Your thoughts...

_____

_____

_____

_____

_____

Gracefully acknowledge everyone you encounter.
Your thoughts...

_____

_____

_____

_____

Choose a good thought each night before you fall asleep.
Your thoughts…

_____

_____

_____

_____

_____

Think of three things you are grateful for before you get out of bed each day.
Your thoughts…

_____

_____

_____

_____

Whose day did you make today?
Your thoughts...

___

Gratitude will change your altitude.
Your thoughts...

___

I love you! Do you?
Your thoughts...

_____
_____
_____
_____
_____

Your thoughts are the script of your life.
Your thoughts...

_____
_____
_____
_____
_____

"*We*" creates glee!
Your thoughts...

_____
_____
_____
_____
_____

If you never fell down, you wouldn't know how

to get up.

Your thoughts...

_____
_____
_____
_____
_____

Even the most "*successful*" people are
carrying around pain.
Your thoughts...

_____

_____

_____

_____

_____

What positive difference did you make today?
Your thoughts...

_____

_____

_____

_____

_____

Being quiet can make the loudest impact.
Your thoughts...

_____
_____
_____
_____
_____

You are greater than you can ever imagine.
Your thoughts...

_____
_____
_____
_____
_____

Even "*stars*" know insecurity.
Your thoughts...

_____
_____
_____
_____
_____

Your greatness is only limited by your thoughts.
Your thoughts...

_____
_____
_____
_____
_____

Ask yourself each day –

"What is my highest and best use?"
Your thoughts...

_____

_____

_____

_____

_____

Praying is asking. Meditating is listening.
Your thoughts...

_____

_____

_____

_____

_____

Every prayer is heard.
Your thoughts...

_____
_____
_____
_____
_____

Wanting is not the same as allowing.
Your thoughts...

_____
_____
_____
_____
_____

List three ways you expressed joy today.
Your thoughts…

_____
_____
_____
_____
_____

You are always just one thought away from
Source.
Your thoughts…

_____
_____
_____
_____
_____

Radiate love to all whom you encounter.
Your thoughts…

_____
_____
_____
_____
_____

You control the energy of every room you enter.
Your thoughts…

_____
_____
_____
_____
_____

Good vibrations are contagious.

Your thoughts...

_____

_____

_____

_____

_____

Assess. Own. Act!

Your thoughts...

_____

_____

_____

_____

_____

Give yourself love first.
Your thoughts...

___

You can't be hurt... unless you choose to be.
Your thoughts...

Thought = Outcome.

Your thoughts…

_____
_____
_____
_____
_____

Saying "*No*" liberates you.

Your thoughts…

_____
_____
_____
_____
_____

Note one way you loved unconditionally today.
Your thoughts...

_____
_____
_____
_____
_____

Love is *always* reciprocated.
Your thoughts...

_____
_____
_____
_____
_____

You are being watched and cared for right at this very moment.
Your thoughts...

_____
_____
_____
_____
_____

You have been specially chosen for this life you are leading.
Your thoughts...

_____
_____
_____
_____

Being in the "*zone*" is alignment with your purpose.
Your thoughts...

_____
_____
_____
_____
_____

Your #1 goal is to live a life of joy.
Your thoughts...

_____
_____
_____
_____
_____

Judging diminishes you.
Your thoughts…

_____
_____
_____
_____
_____

Remove "*but*" from your vocabulary.
Your thoughts…

_____
_____
_____
_____
_____

Things can never go "*wrong.*"
Your thoughts...

_____

_____

_____

_____

_____

What was your listening to talking ratio today?
Your thoughts...

_____

_____

_____

_____

_____

You have 7 billion brothers and sisters you haven't met... yet.
Your thoughts...

_____
_____
_____
_____
_____

Borders are much more than physical barriers.
Your thoughts...

_____
_____
_____
_____
_____

List three reasons why you are a success.
Your thoughts...

_____
_____
_____
_____
_____

Success isn't a linear path.
Your thoughts...

_____
_____
_____
_____
_____

The outside world is not your judge and jury.
Your thoughts...

_____
_____
_____
_____
_____

Vulnerability leads to growth, not hurt.
Your thoughts...

_____
_____
_____
_____
_____

You are loved beyond belief!
Your thoughts...

_____

_____

_____

_____

_____

Send a note of thanks to someone in the public eye who has influenced you.
Your thoughts...

_____

_____

_____

_____

_____

God isn't "*somewhere,*" He is "*everywhere.*"
Your thoughts…

___

Possessions are simply things we hide behind.
Your thoughts…

You are a graceful human "*being*."
Your thoughts...

_____
_____
_____
_____
_____

Hug three people today... it will change their life... and yours.
Your thoughts...

_____
_____
_____
_____
_____

What one thing can you do today to raise your level of awareness?
Your thoughts...

_____
_____
_____
_____
_____

You are a great adventurer on this trip called
"life."
Your thoughts...

_____
_____
_____
_____

In the end, you will laugh at the silly "*you*" who worried.
Your thoughts...

_____

_____

_____

_____

_____

Your supporting cast is so much larger than any Hollywood star's.
Your thoughts...

_____

_____

_____

_____

The so-called "*lowliest*" position may well be the most important.
Your thoughts...

_____
_____
_____
_____
_____

What one thing can you do today to move forward?
Your thoughts...

_____
_____
_____
_____

Everything happens for a reason... and they are all good.
Your thoughts...

_____
_____
_____
_____
_____

Treat each day as a wild adventure.
Your thoughts...

_____
_____
_____
_____
_____

Repeat after me: "*I am a gift to others. I am a gift to others....*"
Your thoughts...

_____

_____

_____

_____

_____

Question... yet never doubt.
Your thoughts...

_____

_____

_____

_____

_____

Always wait two seconds before you answer any question.
Your thoughts...

_____
_____
_____
_____
_____

Try communicating with your heart and see what happens.
Your thoughts...

_____
_____
_____
_____

List ten reasons why you are beautiful.
Your thoughts…

_____
_____
_____
_____
_____

Seek out those who appear to be the
opposite of you.
Your thoughts…

_____
_____
_____
_____
_____

Speak to your fears in a mirror. *Poof!* They disappear.
Your thoughts…

_____

_____

_____

_____

_____

Lack does not really exist.
Your thoughts…

_____

_____

_____

_____

_____

Money does not define you.
Your thoughts...

_____
_____
_____
_____
_____

Every new norm was at one point unheard of.
Your thoughts...

_____
_____
_____
_____
_____

Smile and hold one person's gaze for five seconds today.
Your thoughts...

_____
_____
_____
_____

Imagine yourself wrapped in a blanket of love every day.
Your thoughts...

_____
_____
_____
_____

Seek nature. All answers reside there.

Your thoughts…

_____

_____

_____

_____

_____

There are no zero sum scenarios.

Your thoughts…

_____

_____

_____

_____

_____

Every outcome is within your control.

Your thoughts...

_____

_____

_____

_____

_____

Visualization = Realization.

Your thoughts...

_____

_____

_____

_____

_____

"*Awakening*" should be your highest desire.
Your thoughts...

___

Know that, in the dark nights of the soul, you hold the light.
Your thoughts...

Learn to laugh at so-called "*challenges.*"
Your thoughts...

_____
_____
_____
_____
_____

List three ways you've changed for the better this year.
Your thoughts...

_____
_____
_____
_____
_____

If you learn to forgive, you have lived your purpose.

Your thoughts...

_____

_____

_____

_____

_____

About Drayton

Greetings! I am Drayton Boylston. I'm searching for the answers to the *BIG* questions in life. Since you've found this book, you may be searching as well.

I write and teach about this amazing (and sometimes scary) spiritual adventure we are all on. I am simply here to help shed some light, provide some love, and put my arms around you and let you know that everything will be alright.

Do you wonder why you are here? What your purpose is? Maybe why you aren't feeling fulfilled?

Yep, I was too. That is why I started *Whispers From Your Soul...* to help myself figure these things out. Now, I'm on a mission to help others along this path.

I am so very fortunate to be an internationally respected Speaker, Author, Coach, and now... Spiritual Adventurer. It is so cool that

I can now use my background and experiences to serve others who are seeking answers - just like I was.

I am driven by the *Whispers From My Soul* that took me years to truly hear... and heed. I now <u>share these with you in my blog.</u>

While I had a crazy good ride in the corporate world as a former CEO and Fortune 100 executive, I am now blazing a much different trail over the second half of my life. This new trail of spiritual discovery has led me to shift my entire focus to help others along their own spiritual adventure. I see so much beauty in the gifts I have been given. My buttoned up corporate, *"A,"* driver self now sees the *"other side"* of life. I now know exactly why I have been blessed with my unique journey.

I used to be one of those guys who didn't *"get it"* and quite frankly looked at folks who were doing spiritual work as from another planet. Now I know otherwise... or maybe I just joined them on this other plane? ;-)

Just imagine... a big business guy becoming a *"Spiritual Adventurer?!"* I never would have guessed it 10 years ago. Now it is so cool to see how and why my journey has led me to this place. And while it may freak out some of my former colleagues, I know that all of us will eventually meet up in the same place....

Let's be clear up front... I don't have all the answers. What I do have is a sincere desire to help folks seek them. This doesn't have to be *"out there"* and *"woo-woo"* (it seems like it has been for waaay too long.) I want to make this simple and approachable for everyone. My goal is to help people *translate the ethereal into the real*™.

I have had the privilege to teach thousands of beautiful souls in 38 countries... and counting.

My first book - ***Coming UnScrooged!***™ *A Contemporary Classic of Corporate Rescue and Redemption* has garnered high praise from many quarters. With the addition of my bestseller, *A Whisper From Your Soul*™, I am blessed to have joined the ranks of highly respected authors as well. Just a couple of ways that I simply act as a conduit for important messages that I am here to share.

My forthcoming book - *A Boomer's Search For Meaning*™ is sure to shed considerable light on personal spiritual discovery. My hope with this book is that it will bring the spiritual conversation to the mainstream—from coffee shops to board rooms. My desire is to help people unite and collectively bond around these vital conversations.

With the launch of our (it's all of ours!) *Life Meaning Project*™, I want to inspire people all over the world to share their experiences along the path of finding meaning in their lives.

My overarching mission is to help 10 million people *save themselves from the lives they've created*®!

I write and teach from my peaceful mountaintop office at 8,000 ft. up in the Colorado Rockies.

Read more about my journey here:

www.DraytonBoylston.com

I can be reached at
Support@DraytonBoylston.com or
1.800.251.1696.

Media and speaking inquiries please visit:

http://www.draytonboylston.com/programs

Resources

My personal web site where you can read my blog and other musings:

www.DraytonBoylston.com

The Life Meaning Project:

http://www.draytonboylston.com/the-life-meaning-project

The Executive Coaching University:

www.ExecutiveCoachingUniversity.com/

Executive Coaching and Mentoring:

http://www.executivecoachinguniversity.com/coaching-with-the-masters/